W9-ALN-218

DISCARD

HOW TO

TO

IMPROVE YOUR GRAMMAR AND USAGE

HOW TO IMPROVE YOUR GRAMMAR AND USAGE

BY MARK ROWH

A SPEAK OUT, WRITE ON! BOOK
Franklin Watts
New York/Chicago/London/Toronto/Sydney

Library of Congress Cataloging-in-Publication Data

Rowh, Mark.
How to improve your grammar and usage / by Mark Rowh.
p.   cm. — (A Speak out, write on! book)
Includes bibliographical references (p.) and index.
ISBN 0-531-11177-6
1. English language—Grammar.   2. English language—Usage.
[1. English language—Grammar.   2. English language—Usage.]
I. Title.   II. Series.
PE1112.R67   1994
428.2—dc20   93-31276 CIP AC

CONTENTS

This book is dedicated to Evelyn Jeffries, Ray Watkins, William Sullivan, A. M. Tyson, the late Roland Wobbe, and all the other teachers and professors who helped me develop a basic understanding of English grammar and usage.

ONE
WHY GRAMMAR IS IMPORTANT

Is grammar important to you? Before answering, consider the following questions:

1) Have you ever had to write an essay, research paper, report, or business letter?
2) Do you expect to do a lot of writing in college or at a future job?
3) Would you like to feel confident that you are speaking correctly during interviews, oral presentations, or ordinary conversation?
4) Could you stand some improvement in understanding and following the rules that govern the way we communicate?

If you answered "yes" to most or all of these questions, then this book is for you. Maybe you are someone who has always felt weak in this area. Or perhaps you feel somewhat confident about your grammatical skills, but realize you still have some room for improvement. In either case, developing a good grasp of the rules of grammar and usage is important.

"Grammar" may not be the most popular word in the English language, but there is no escaping the fact that the way you speak and write has a major impact on many facets of everyday life. To be successful in communicating, it is vital that you master the basics of grammar and usage.

To get a clear idea of just how important these skills can be, consider the following situations:

SCENARIO 1. A college admissions committee is reviewing applications for the upcoming freshman class. Fewer than half of those who have applied can be admitted, for there is room for only a certain number of students at this prestigious college. As a result, members of the committee find themselves looking for reasons to reject some of the applications. When the next one hits the table, one of the reviewers points out that the application contains several grammatical errors. A colleague agrees, and one committee member suggests that this application be placed in the stack reserved for those to be turned down. No one disagrees, and the application is rejected.

SCENARIO 2. An employer has narrowed down his applicants for a well-paying job to two young women. Their credentials and backgrounds seem roughly equivalent, and he feels either could do the job. But he couldn't help noticing that one woman made a couple of grammatical errors in her letter of application, and used some sloppy grammar during her oral interview. The manager shrugs as he considers the situation, realizing that he has never been a real stickler about grammar himself. But there has to be some basis to choose one over the next, and the position does involve working with the public, where good impressions always count. So he finally tosses aside the application with the grammatical problems, and reaches for the phone to call the other young woman and offer her the job.

SCENARIO 3. It is the first year of college. You have worked hard on a long, complex research paper. Hoping for a grade of at least a "B" and maybe an "A," you anxiously await the results of the instructor's review. To your disappointment, however, the grade comes back a "C." The instructor's main criticism is not about content, for he seems favorably impressed and has written several compliments on your ideas in the margins. But he also notes that your paper was marred by several grammatical errors.

SCENARIO 4. You're walking around the mall when a friend asks to borrow a few dollars. "I don't have no money," you respond. Suddenly the air fills with bullets as uniformed officers start firing in your direction and screaming something about "double negatives." Then you realize—it's the Grammar Police!

Okay, so this last scenario may be a bit exaggerated. But the fact is, we live in a highly judgmental society. No matter who you are, people make all kinds of assessments about you. High school teachers, college professors, employers, professors, potential mothers-in-law, and people you've never even thought about are constantly forming opinions about you—or will do so in the future. Their views will be based on a variety of factors: the way you dress, where you go to school, how you talk, how you write. These last two include that sometimes imposing point of concern, grammar.

To be fair, it is important to realize that grammar is not just a set of arbitrary rules invented by some ancient scholar to drive generations of students crazy. Actually, grammar in the ordinary world operates independently of efforts by linguists, English teachers or anyone else to describe or control it. All languages have certain basic rules that are followed at least to some extent by everyone who speaks them, even those who cannot read or write. For example, the concept of word order is one of the fundamental elements of grammar, and everyone who speaks English understands the basics of putting words in a specific sequence so that they make sense to others (otherwise, people would babble meaningless phrases understandable only to themselves).

What has happened, though, is that society has added the concept of conformity. It is not enough simply to make yourself understood. To be well regarded, you must communicate in a socially acceptable manner. That means, among other things, demonstrating acceptable grammar and usage. When you think about it, this is the only smart way to go. After all, a person with any savvy does not show up for a job interview in a T-shirt and gym shorts, or take a bath only when the seasons change, or use obscene language when making a class presentation. In the same way, the intelligent person makes certain his or her grammar meets normal expectations.

WHAT GRAMMAR AND USAGE ARE

Before going further, let's stop and develop working definitions of grammar and usage. These words are often used very loosely to describe just about everything having to do with the use of language. But a more narrowly defined approach may be in order.

Look in any comprehensive dictionary, and you will find several definitions of grammar. The *American Heritage Dictionary*, for example, lists the following definitions:

1. The study of language as a systematically composed body of words that exhibit discernible regularity of structure and arrangement into sentences and sometimes including such aspects of language as the pronunciation of words, the meaning of words, and the history of words.
2. a. The phenomena with which grammar deals as exhibited by a specific language at a specific time. b. The system of rules implicit in a language, viewed as a mechanism for generating all sentences possible in that language.
3. A normative or prescriptive system of rules setting forth the current standard of usage for pedagogical or reference purposes.
4. Writing or speech judged with regard to the rules or practice of grammar: (for example) *bad grammar.*
5. A book containing the syntactic and semantic rules for a specific language.
6. a. The basic principles of an area of knowledge: (for example) *the grammar of music.* b. A book dealing with such principles.

While this may seem complicated, the third and fourth definitions are the truly important ones, at least for our purposes here. In other words, grammar as discussed in this book means all the rules that govern how we put words together to communicate, as well as the overall effects of applying those rules.

Usage, on the other hand, refers to the process of choosing and using words correctly. *Webster's School Dictionary* defines usage as follows:

1a. a firmly established and generally accepted practice or procedure

1b. the way in which words and phrases are actually used in a language community
2a. the action or mode of using: use
2b. manner of treating: treatment.

The first definition applies most directly to the purposes of this book. Usage, as discussed here, refers not just to how words and phrases are commonly used but to how they *should* be used (in other terms, to what is acceptable). For instance, a phrase such as "most unique" may represent common usage, but not *correct* usage. It is the latter that will be emphasized in chapter 6.

All of us need to understand the basic grammatical rules and usage practices of the English language, and be able to apply them with ease and consistency. Sound hard? It really isn't, but one can understand why this multifaceted task may appear difficult.

WHY GRAMMAR SEEMS DIFFICULT

To many people, mastering effective grammar seems a formidable task. The process means learning a large number of rules and then applying them in all kinds of situations.

In some ways, this is similar to absorbing *any* set of rules. Learning how to play chess, for instance, means you must gain an understanding of how each piece moves, what moves are allowable, and what is prohibited. Once you master these rules, you can play the game.

When it comes to the English language, however, things get complicated. This is due in part to the fact that English is a language based on many influences. You have probably read that America has been considered a melting pot of different cultures due to heavy immigration from other nations. In a similar way, English represents a mix of different languages. Along with these different languages have come rules and practices that are not always consistent. English has been heavily influenced by French, Latin, and other languages. Incorporating such influences along with original characteristics of the Anglo-Saxon language (the forerunner of modern English), our language has become rather complex.

The combination of languages contributing to English has contributed to an extensive vocabulary of more than one million words, probably the largest of any major language in the world. This means, among other things, that there is more room to make an error, or at least a bad choice, in some aspect of usage or grammar. Nevertheless, that does not mean you should feel overwhelmed. On the contrary, anyone can succeed with the right approach.

WHY IT DOESN'T HAVE TO BE THAT HARD

Maybe you have always hated English classes and everything that goes with them. Perhaps the word *grammar* sends shivers running through your soul. Or maybe it is nothing that dramatic, but you have never felt confident about your own grammatical skills.

Regardless of your background, if you buy the theory that grammar is important, you will agree that some effort toward improvement will be worthwhile. The next step, then, is to do something about making those needed improvements.

What you may not realize, though, is that mastering good grammar and usage need not be an overwhelming task.

Why? Because you can succeed by concentrating on the basics. We are not saying that you have to become a fanatic about grammar to succeed in life. Nobody is recommending that you become a perfect writer and speaker. You do not have to become an

English teacher's dream student, or a counterpart to "Star Trek" 's precise Mr. Spock. All you really must do is develop a basic understanding of major grammatical rules and concepts, and then apply them consistently.

This might be compared to learning how to shoot a lay-up in basketball. At first it takes some effort to master the basic elements of this fundamental shot: getting your steps down, learning how to release the ball softly and roll it off your fingertips, and controlling the flight of the ball so that it travels just the right distance at just the right speed. You may misfire at first, but with practice almost anyone can learn to shoot a lay-up. That's one of the basic elements of basketball.

Now picture Michael Jordan soaring through the air and jamming the ball home. That's much more than basics. Such talents may be wonderful, but they are not necessary for the average person who just wants to play a little basketball.

Dealing with grammar and usage is the same thing. You don't have to be the Michael Jordan of grammar. By mastering a few basic principles, you can function effectively and give yourself some real advantages in a highly competitive world.

USING THIS BOOK

This is the end of the sales pitch. If you do not believe by now that grammar and usage are important, perhaps you never will. If, on the other hand, you agree that you can benefit by polishing your own skills in these two areas, read on and see how paying attention to a few basic concepts can help.

Chapter 2 covers major grammatical errors and how to avoid them. Do you know which grammatical errors are considered the most serious, and how you can make sure they don't cause you problems? This chapter will provide the answers in simple, understandable terms.

Chapter 3 will help you handle adjectives and adverbs easily and effectively, and Chapter 4 covers verbs. These sections include examples of incorrect applications, why they are wrong, and preferred alternatives.

Chapter 5 discusses the use of nouns and pronouns. This includes tips for making sense of the proper case to use and the correct form of nouns and pronouns within sentences.

The sixth chapter covers appropriate usage, emphasizing common usage problems and ways to avoid them. A list of frequently confused words and phrases is included.

Chapter 7 concludes the book with advice on continuing the learning process and making an ongoing commitment to effective grammar and usage.

In proceeding from here, remember these two major concepts: (1) Good grammar is vital for success not only in school but also in the "real world" of work and in various kinds of interpersonal communication, and (2) you need not memorize a million rules and spend your weekends diagramming sentences to develop good grammatical skills. Rather, understanding a few basic principles and developing a pragmatic approach to grammar and usage can help anyone master this important area.

TWO

AVOIDING MAJOR GRAMMATICAL PROBLEMS

Some elements of grammar and usage are more critical to clear communication than others. For example, if an immigrant whose native language is not English says something like "give me book," most American listeners would understand what is meant. The lack of the article "the" from the more complete statement of "give me the book" does not destroy the overall meaning.

Leaving out the pronoun "me," on the other hand, might distort the basic meaning. In saying "give book," the speaker could mean "give me the book" or "I will give you the book," among other possibilities.

For people who have spoken English since infancy, expectations are generally higher that the finer points of grammar will be observed. Yet even for native English speakers, a certain hierarchy exists in terms of grammatical priorities. Some elements of grammar are more important than others. Conversely, some grammatical mistakes are more serious than others.

While there is no definitive system for determining the relative importance of such elements, most English teachers and other "experts" would rate the following as among the most serious grammatical errors:

Sentence fragments
Run-on sentences
Comma splices
Errors in subject-verb agreement

By avoiding these serious errors, anyone can go a long way toward achieving a solid mastery of English grammar. Following is an overview of these basic errors, and how you can avoid or eliminate them from your own work.

SENTENCE FRAGMENTS

A sentence fragment is a group of words that does not qualify as a complete sentence even though the writer has intended it to fulfill this function. A complete sentence must have the following elements:

1) It must have a *subject*.
2) It must have a *verb*.
3) It must express a *complete thought* without dependency on other sentences.
4) It must be followed by some type of *end punctuation*.

This sounds simple enough, but as is true of many elements of grammar, some additional explanation is needed. For instance, a subject can be missing from a sentence if it is considered to be "understood," as in these examples:

Pick up the trash.
Wait until the light changes.

In both examples, the subject is understood to be "you," and the statements are still considered to be complete sentences. Similarly, an exclamation such as "No!" can function as a sentence.

Aside from these generally recognized exceptions, however, a sentence is not considered to be complete if one of the four elements listed above is missing. When a key element is missing, the result is a significant error. Among the most serious of these mistakes are "sentence fragments."

A sentence fragment is an incomplete sentence. A fragment becomes a problem when one attempts to use it as a complete sentence.

An analogy might be the use of counterfeit money. It may look like real money, but spending a fake bill can land you in jail. Using sentence fragments might not be against the law, but many English teachers would say this weakness is almost as bad!

Whatever you do, make sure you avoid the dreaded sentence fragment in your own writing. Learn to recognize fragments and to be on the alert for any instance where they might creep unintentionally into your own work.

Here is a typical example of a sentence fragment:

Tim quit the team. Because the coach did not seem to like him.

The second group of words is not a sentence, even though it contains a subject and a verb. The word "because" is the culprit; it makes this group of words subordinate to (or dependent on) the first one. Standing on its own, the phrase "Because the coach did not seem to like him" does not convey a complete thought.

To revise this statement (or any other sentence fragment), you can take either of the following steps:

1) Combine the fragment and another sentence into a single, complete sentence.
2) Turn the fragment into a sentence by adding or deleting words as necessary.

Either step will work, but the process of revision may require some analysis and perhaps a little creativity. Following are some alternative approaches and the thinking behind them.

> *Tim quit the team. The coach did not seem to like him.*

In this case, the second statement is no longer a fragment. Simply deleting the word "because" changes the situation so that the second statement is no longer dependent on the first one. At the same time, this may not be the best possible revision, for the two sentences may not be sufficiently linked to convey fully the writer's intended meaning.

Some simple rewording (possibly retaining the word "because," but with a different organizational pattern) may make a more effective revision, as in these examples:

> *Tim quit the team because the coach did not seem to like him.*

This combines what had been one sentence and one fragment into a single, longer, but still coherent sentence.

> *Because the coach did not seem to like him, Tim quit the team.*

This revision also combines what had been two statements into one, while at the same time inverting their order without changing the meaning (note that a comma has been added since "Because the coach did not seem to like him" now serves as an introductory phrase).

The coach did not seem to like him, so Tom quit the team.

Here, "so" is used instead of "because," and a single sentence results from the combination of what had previously been two separate statements.

All sentence fragments are not the result of the failure to recognize that one clause is dependent on another. Many come about when a phrase is mistaken for a sentence, either through misunderstanding or simple carelessness. If either a subject or a verb is missing, a phrase does not meet the definition of a sentence. Here are some examples, along with possible revisions:

Not acceptable:	*The cowboys started celebrating. Shooting their guns into the air.*
Reason:	*The second statement is not a sentence. It lacks a complete subject-verb relationship, since the word "shooting" is not accompanied by another word that would establish such a relationship.*
Acceptable:	*The cowboys started celebrating and shooting their guns into the air.*
Reason:	*The statements have been combined into a single sentence that includes all the elements required of a sentence.*
Acceptable:	*The cowboys started celebrating. They began shooting their guns into the air.*
Reason:	*The addition of the verb "began" in the second statement makes it an acceptable sentence, with a complete subject-verb relationship.*

Not acceptable:	*The Tigers finished their season with a flourish. Winning six games in a row.*
Reason:	*The second group of words is not a sentence. There is no subject, and "winning," as used here, cannot serve on its own as the verb in the sentence.*
Acceptable:	*The Tigers finished their season with a flourish by winning six games in a row.*
Reason:	*The revised statement contains a subject and a verb, and a complete thought, all expressed within a single sentence.*

Other examples of fragments and some possible revisions are as follows:

Not acceptable:	*It was the knife. The one which had been used in the murder.*
Reason:	*The second group of words may look like a sentence, but it is not. If you cover the preceding sentence with your hand or a piece of paper, this fact becomes more obvious. To what does the noun "the one" refer? Its meaning is linked to the complete sentence, "It was the knife." As constructed, the second group of words does not stand on its own with a complete subject-verb relationship.*
Acceptable:	*It was the knife, the one that had been used in the murder.*
Reason:	*In this version, no attempt is made to develop or simulate a second sen-*

tence. Instead, the same thirteen words have been grouped into a single, acceptable sentence.

Acceptable: *It was the knife that had been used in the murder.*

Reason: *This version may be an improvement. It conveys the same information in fewer words, and without any punctuation needed other than the period at the end of the sentence.*

Not acceptable: *Jenny got to fly in a jet fighter. And even to take a turn at the controls.*

Reason: *Who was allowed to take a turn at the controls? Even though the second group of words may make basic sense, it lacks the elements of a complete sentence, and would not make the same sense if isolated from the sentence that precedes it.*

Acceptable: *Jenny got to ride in a jet fighter, and even to take a turn at the controls.*

Reason: *As a single unified sentence, this version contains the necessary elements of a sentence, thanks to the addition of the word "and."*

Acceptable: *Jenny got to ride in a jet fighter. She even took a turn at the controls.*

Learning to recognize sentence fragments is one of the fundamental steps anyone can take in avoiding grammatical problems. If you spot a fragment in your own work—or even suspect that a statement might be a fragment—be sure to rephrase your thought so that only solid, complete sentences are used.

Within limits, the use of fragments may be acceptable. In fact, skilled writers sometimes employ fragments to achieve a conversational tone or other desired effect. Following are some examples of this practice:

No problem. We can ship the order to your home within a week of your request.

If you think taking drugs is worth the risk, you may be wrong. Dead wrong.

In the first example, the commonly spoken phrase "no problem" takes the place of a sentence, at the same time making written communication seem chatty and informal. This can be effective in sales literature or other applications where the writer wants to avoid sounding stiff or formal.

The second example helps achieve a certain dramatic effect. By inserting the phrase "dead wrong" where one would expect a complete sentence, the writer emphasizes the word "dead" in a way that might not otherwise be possible. The result is enhanced potential for making an impact on the reader.

In cases such as those cited above, fragments can be used effectively. This is only true, however, when the writer is totally aware that a fragment is being utilized, and the reader is not prompted to wonder whether the use of a fragment was intentional. Another necessary condition is that the writing be intended for informal use. In highly formal writing (such as research papers, legal documents, and formal business letters), fragments are generally considered to be unacceptable, even if intentional.

In any other instance, sentence fragments should not be used. In fact, unless you are a very skilled writer with a deep understanding of grammatical rules, the best approach is to stay away from fragments altogether.

FUSED SENTENCES

A fused sentence occurs when two sentences are joined together as if they were a single sentence, but without the use of appropriate punctuation or wording. This is also known as a run-on sentence.

Like fragments, fused sentences represent very serious errors. They seem to indicate that the writer does not understand the basic nature of a sentence.

Fused sentences tend to be more obvious than fragments, and therefore might not be considered easier to use. At any rate, they should always be avoided.

Here are some examples of fused sentences, as well as corrected versions.

Not acceptable: *He hit me in the jaw I hit him right back.*

Acceptable: *He hit me in the jaw. I hit him right back.*

Acceptable: *He hit me in the jaw, and I hit him right back.*

Not acceptable: *The show is wonderful everyone should see it.*

Acceptable: *The show is wonderful. Everyone should see it.*

Acceptable: *The show is wonderful! Everyone should see it.*

Acceptable: *The show is so wonderful that everyone should see it.*

Not Acceptable: *Benny gave her the money she deserved it.*

Acceptable: *Benny gave her the money. She deserved it.*

Acceptable: *Benny gave her the money; she deserved it.*

Acceptable: *Benny gave her the money because she deserved it.*

If all this seems too obvious for discussion, good for you. But fused sentences are an all-too-common problem, a fact to which many high school teachers and instructors of college English composition classes can attest. Make sure that your own writing is not weakened by fused sentences.

COMMA SPLICES

One of the most important rules of grammar is as follows: Never use a comma to join two sentences together. This is known as a comma splice. It is to be avoided at all times.

Here are some examples of comma splices:

The report is almost finished, it will be ready this afternoon.

Mr. Smith must have been surprised by the remark, he seemed to lose his composure for a few seconds.

This paint job is unacceptable, the color is too bright.

Jan failed the exam, she will be allowed to take it again.

In each case, the material that appears before the comma could stand on its own as a complete sentence, and the same is true of the words following the comma. Both statements in each example qualify as what is known as a main clause (or independent clause). This is a group of words that contains both a subject and a verb and could function as a complete sentence by itself.

At first glance, comma splices may not seem to be horrendous errors, but they actually are among the most serious that can be made. Why is this so? The answer may be that comma splices lead the reader to believe that the writer does not understand exactly what constitutes a sentence. Since the sentence is such a fundamental element of language, this hints at a kind of grammatical illiteracy. If you do not know how to write an acceptable sentence, according to this line of thinking, you may be grossly inadequate in your mastery of grammar.

Of course, the use of comma splices may not mean this at all. Perhaps the writer simply has been careless. Or maybe this matter has not previously been called to the writer's attention. At any rate, comma splices are relatively easy to avoid. They also can be readily "fixed" once they have occurred.

Following are some basic approaches for correcting comma splices.

Approach No. 1. *Replace the comma with a period.* If you remove the comma from a comma splice and replace it with a period, your problem is solved. Here are two examples:

Not acceptable: *The new player was obviously nervous, he missed several easy shots. The pizza is too cold, I will heat it in the microwave.*

Acceptable: *The new player was obviously nervous. He missed several easy shots. The pizza is too cold. I will heat it in the microwave.*

By breaking what had previously been a single sentence into two shorter sentences, the comma splice has been eliminated in each instance.

This technique works adequately, but it may not be the best choice if the resulting sentences are too short, because the writing comes across as too choppy or abrupt. Much depends on the length of other sentences in the same passage and an overall sense of balance. On the other hand, correct sentences of any length are always preferred to comma splices.

Approach No. 2. *Replace the comma with a semicolon.* Another method is to delete the comma and replace it with a semicolon, as shown below.

Not acceptable:	*Bring your own lunch, soft drinks and coffee will be provided.*
	Ryan's arm seemed to be broken, it just dangled by his side.
Acceptable:	*Bring your own lunch; soft drinks and coffee will be provided.*
	Ryan's arm seemed to be broken; it just dangled from his side.

Different rules govern the use of the comma and the semicolon. The latter may be used to join statements which could stand on their own as sentences, and there is no such thing as a "semicolon splice"! In the examples shown here, the statements are joined in a way that matches what the writer originally intended, but that doesn't violate the rules.

A danger in using semicolons is that you must understand their correct use and avoid inappropriate applications. For example, be careful to avoid confusing the semicolon (;) with the colon (:). To be safe, consult a reference book on punctuation.

Approach No. 3. *Add a word or phrase that helps relate the two thoughts being expressed.* A comma alone is insufficient for linking two sentences, but the addition of a single word can do the trick. Consider these examples:

Not acceptable:	*He is a happy person, he smiles all the time.*
Reason:	*Each of the two statements can function as a complete sentence. Joining*

Acceptable: these two independent clauses with a comma results in a comma splice.
He is a happy person, and he smiles all the time.

Reason: The addition of the word "and" ties the two statements together in an acceptable fashion. "And" is known as a coordinating conjunction; its function is to join together words or groups of words that are considered equal in grammatical terms (such as one sentence to another). Since the purpose of a conjunction is to function as this type of connector, the overall result is that it follows the rules of grammar, and a comma splice no longer exists.

In addition to "and," other coordinating conjunctions include:

but   or
for   yet
nor

Any of these words can be used to join clauses that could otherwise stand alone as complete sentences.

Acceptable: Because he is a happy person, he smiles all the time.

Reason: The addition of "because" not only ties the two thoughts together but also changes the thrust of the first statement. "Because he is a happy person" is not a main or independent clause; the statement depends on another sentence for its meaning to be complete. Thus, the elements *that make up a comma splice no longer exist.*

"Because" is a conjunction, but unlike "and" and the others listed above, its purpose is to help show that one idea is dependent on (or subordinate to) another. Such words are known as subordinating conjunctions. They can help establish relationships such as time, cause, and effect, or contrast. In addition to "because," other subordinating conjunctions include:

as	since
as if	until
after	while
before	when
if	

Subordinating conjunctions should be used with care. While they can help to "fix" a comma splice, they can also lead to sentence fragments if a clause that includes a coordinating conjunction is left to function alone as a sentence. The key point to remember is that their purpose is to *connect*, and you should use them in that fashion.

Approach No. 4. *Rephrase one or both statements.* An alternative to the approaches described thus far is simply to use different wording. You can delete words, add words, or change word order, among other options.

Not acceptable:	*David had not read the lesson, he did not know what to say.*
Reason:	*As with the previous examples, this is not acceptable because it uses a comma to combine two main clauses; each can function as a complete sentence.*

Acceptable:	*David, who had not read the lesson, did not know what to say.*
Reason:	*What had been two sentences has now been combined into a single sentence with a single subject.*
Acceptable:	*David did not know what to say. He had not read the lesson.*
Reason:	*The order of the two statements has been reversed, and each is presented as a complete sentence with periods used instead of a comma.*

THE "HOWEVER" PROBLEM

Among the most common comma splices are those involving the word "however" and other words that operate in a similar fashion. In fact, many people with better-than-average grammatical skills fail to understand the proper way to link clauses using such words.

The essence of this problem is that "however" and other such words cannot be used to link sentences with only a comma. "However" is not a coordinating conjunction such as "but" or "and," but rather a conjunctive adverb. As such, it can be used at different points within a sentence, as in the following examples:

Lisa, however, felt differently.
The game was a long and close one; however, the home team finally prevailed.

If used to connect two main clauses, as in the second example, "however" should be preceded by a semicolon, and is usually followed by a comma. This is illustrated by the following:

Not acceptable:	*She wanted the job very much, however, she had no related work experience.*

Acceptable:	*She wanted the job very much; however, she had no related work experience.*
Not acceptable:	*The argument might have been avoided, however, perhaps it was all for the best.*
Acceptable:	*The argument might have been avoided; however, perhaps it was all for the best.*

Other conjunctive adverbs include:

besides
consequently
finally
furthermore
meanwhile
nevertheless
still
therefore

If one of these words is used to combine two sentences with a comma rather than a semicolon, a comma splice will result.

An alternative to using a semicolon is to create two sentences instead of one. This also will help avoid comma splices, as shown in these statements:

Not acceptable:	*He is guilty, therefore, he should be punished.*
Acceptable:	*He is guilty; therefore, he should be punished.*
Acceptable:	*He is guilty. Therefore, he should be punished.*

Transitional phrases such as "in conclusion," "for example," "after all," "in addition," "in fact," "on the other hand," and others that establish similar transitions should be handled in the same manner, as in the following examples:

Not acceptable: *Many people don't understand what causes comma splices, as a result, their writing may suffer.*

Acceptable: *Many people don't understand what causes comma splices; as a result, their writing may suffer.*

Acceptable: *Many people don't understand what causes comma splices. As a result, their writing may suffer.*

Not acceptable: *The economy is in bad shape, in fact, some economists feel a depression is inevitable.*

Acceptable: *The economy is in bad shape; in fact, some economists feel a depression is inevitable.*

Acceptable: *The economy is in bad shape. In fact, some economists feel a depression is inevitable.*

SUBJECT-VERB AGREEMENT

Another area in which mistakes can be particularly serious is that of subject-verb agreement. The underlying concept here is consistency. The subject and verb of a sentence should correspond: single subjects should have single verbs, and plural subjects should have plural verbs. Failing to achieve proper subject-verb agreement is a serious shortcoming in written or spoken communication.

The following sentence *does not* demonstrate correct subject-verb agreement:

The dogs is filthy.

Of course, the correct version would be:

The dogs are filthy.

A plural subject needs a plural verb, and a singular subject takes a singular verb. This may seem obvious, but sometimes the distinction is not as clear-cut as in the example cited above. Sometimes another noun is mistaken for the subject, and the writer or speaker then uses the wrong form of the verb. In some cases, there may be confusion about whether a noun is singular or plural. For a variety of reasons, errors in subject-verb agreement are common. If you can avoid them, your mastery of grammar will be significantly enhanced.

THE "S" FACTOR

For many nouns, adding the suffix "s" makes the word plural. The same is true of "es" for some words. For many verbs, on the other hand, adding "s" or "es" makes the verb singular as in these examples:

The boy runs ("boy" is a singular subject, and "runs" is a singular verb).

The boys run ("boys" is a plural subject, and "run" is a plural verb).

The apple tastes good ("apple" is a singular subject, and "tastes" is a singular verb).

The apples taste good ("apples" is a plural subject, and "taste" is a plural verb).

What might be called the "s" factor is a helpful signal in watching for errors in subject-verb agreement. If both the subject and the verb end in "s" or "es," look carefully to make sure an agreement error has not been made. This is not always the case, for some words end naturally in "s" or "es" even though they are not plural (such as "mathematics"). For nouns in which "s" or "es" is a suffix indicating they are plural, though, the accompanying verb should also be plural.

COMPLICATING FACTORS

The matter of subject-verb agreement is sometimes more complex than might first appear because of the complicated nature of many sentences. In very simple sentences such as those used as examples above, it is not difficult to pick out the subjects and verbs, and then determine if they agree properly. Many sentences, however, contain additional elements that can make it more difficult to handle this matter correctly. Intervening phrases, compound subjects, inverted word order, and other factors must be taken into account in order to achieve proper subject-verb agreement. Here are examples of some typical situations and the rules that apply to them:

Not acceptable: *The list of expired dates are long.*
Acceptable: *The list of expired dates is long.*
Reason: *The subject of this sentence is "list,"*
                   not "dates." Accordingly, a singular
                   verb ("is") should be used. As a rule,
                   the subject of a sentence will not be
                   found within a prepositional phrase
                   (such as "to the store," "after the
                   war," and other phrases consisting
                   of a preposition and an object).
Not acceptable: *Alex and Mike always handles the money.*
Acceptable: *Alex and Mike always handle the money.*

Reason:	*The subject of this sentence is plural, not singular, because two nouns have been joined by "and." Thus, a singular verb is appropriate.*
Not acceptable:	*Either Alex or Mike always handle the money.*
Acceptable:	*Either Alex or Mike always handles the money.*
Reason:	*"Or" is used differently than "and." It does not join words together, but differentiates between them. One or the other (Mike or Alex) does the action, but not both. Thus, a singular verb is correct. The same principle applies to the use of "neither" and "nor."*
Not acceptable:	*Neither the dog nor the two cats has fleas.*
Acceptable:	*Neither the dog nor the two cats have fleas.*
Reason:	*This is one of this situations that arise in grammar where a rather arbitrary rule applies. Unlike the previous example about Alex and Mike, "nor" does not serve to differentiate between two singular subjects. Instead, one subject is singular, and the other is plural. When this happens, the noun placed closer to the verb is used to determine whether the singular or plural form of the verb should be used. In this instance, the plural word "cats" is closer to the verb than the singular word "dog," so the use of a plural verb ("have") is correct. If the word order of "dog" and "cats" had been reversed, a sin-*

gular verb would have been appropriate, as in this example:

Neither the two cats nor the dog has fleas.

Not acceptable: *Terri, along with several other girls in the cast, have broken down with the measles.*

Acceptable: *Terri, along with several other girls in the cast, has broken down with the measles.*

Reason: *When a phrase such as "along with" comes after a singular subject, a singular verb is used. For purposes of subject-verb agreement, this complementary phrase should be disregarded. Other phrases for which this rule applies include "as well as," "in addition to," "not to mention," and "together with."*

While the factors discussed here may make subject-verb agreement seem complex, you can simplify the matter by taking these steps:

1) Identify the subject of the sentence in question. In the process, rule out other words that might be confused with the subject.
2) Determine if the subject is singular or plural.
3) Identify the verb that corresponds to the subject.
4) Make sure the verb agrees with the subject.

THREE

HANDLING ADJECTIVES AND ADVERBS

Adjectives and adverbs add flair to our spoken and written language. Without them, the ability to communicate would be severely limited. Color, size, speed, and many other concepts would be difficult or impossible to relate.

As an illustration of the importance of descriptive language, consider the following statement:

Linda wore a dress.

There is nothing grammatically wrong with this statement, but does it convey enough information? Upon reading this sentence, most people would like to know more. They would expect details such as the following:

Linda wore a light blue dress.
Linda wore a simple, white summer dress.
Linda wore a short, flimsy white dress with red polka dots.

Or consider a statement such as this:

The soldier walked up the hill.

Wouldn't it be good to know *how* the soldier walked? The addition of a single word could make a major difference, as in these examples:

> *The soldier walked slowly up the hill.*
> *The soldier walked confidently up the hill.*
> *The soldier walked tentatively up the hill.*

Descriptive language not only enhances communication, but in many cases is necessary to convey an idea fully. Often this is accomplished through the use of adjectives and adverbs.

While adjectives and adverbs may be desirable, they can also bring problems. Using an adjective when an adverb is called for, for example, is a common mistake. This can make an unfavorable impression on the intended audience.

The rules governing the use of adjectives and adverbs are not especially complicated, and should not lead to major problems in your own writing or speaking. As with other aspects of grammar and usage, serious problems can be avoided if you develop a basic understanding of the way adjectives and adverbs work.

THREE COMMON PROBLEMS TO AVOID

Although the rules governing adjectives and adverbs may be less complicated than those applied to other grammatical concepts, they must be followed closely or errors will result. Following is an overview of three common errors that should be avoided.

Confusing Adjectives and Adverbs

One of the most common problems in using adjectives and adverbs is to use one mistakenly when the other should apply.

An *adjective* is most frequently used to modify a *noun* (most nouns are persons, places or things; for a more complete definition, see chapter 5). The first word in each of the following examples is an adjective:

pretty girl
hungry animal
red car
careless driver

Adjectives can also modify pronouns. They also may originate from other parts of speech or function as other parts of speech depending on the situation (for example, "frightened" is sometimes a verb, but it can also be an adjective, as in "the frightened child").

An *adverb* is used most often to modify a *verb* (most verbs convey action; see Chapter 4 for a more complete definition). The second word in each of the following examples is an adverb:

sobbed uncontrollably
sang loudly
ate quickly
performed well

Adverbs can also be used to describe or limit adjectives, other adverbs, or even entire sentences. Here is an example of the latter:

Sadly, the entire crew perished ("sadly" is an adverb modifying the whole sentence).

In some cases, a group of words may function as an adverb, but more commonly an adverb is a single word.

In effective writing or speaking, it is important to distinguish between adverbs and adjectives as one makes word choices. The first step in making a correct choice between an adjective and an adverb is to look at the word being described and determine whether it is a noun, verb, or some other part of speech. Then

Table 3-1

Some Representative Adjectives and Adverbs

Adjective	*Adverb*
bad	badly
beautiful	beautifully
common	commonly
deep	deep or deeply
different	differently
easy	easily
full	fully
good	well
happy	happily
helpful	helpfully
loud	loud or loudly
perfect	perfectly
probable	probably
real	really
shy	shyly
slow	slow or slowly
soft	softly

select the proper adjective or adverb to accomplish the desired description.

For many words, the easiest way to distinguish between an adjective and an adverb is the addition of the suffix "ly" to the latter. Such words function as adjectives without "ly," and as adverbs if "ly" is added. Examples include "careful" and "carefully," "deep" and "deeply," "happy" and "happily," and "stupid" and "stupidly." Even though this is the most typical pattern, however, it is not the only one. For example, a few adjectives (such as "deadly" and "timely" end in "ly") even though they are not adverbs, and some words can function as either adjectives or adverbs (for example, one might encounter a "cowardly" lion, or a person could act "cowardly").

A typical adjective might comment on the appearance, size, or quality of the noun or pronoun in question. A typical adverb might convey descriptions such as how, where, or when an action takes place, among other concepts.

If you are unsure about a word and whether it has been properly used as an adjective or an adverb, consult a good dictionary. The *American Heritage Dictionary*, for instance, not only gives information on parts of speech but also provides usage notes to help you decide how best to use words.

Some representative adjectives and adverbs are listed in Table 3-1 on page 42. A few examples of proper choices between adverbs and adjectives follow:

Not acceptable:	*The new paint matched perfect with the old color.*
Reason:	*"Perfect" is an adjective, but the intent here is to modify the verb "matched," describing* how *or* how well *the paint matched. Thus, an adverb is needed, not an adjective.*
Acceptable:	*The new paint matched perfectly with the old color.*
Reason:	*The adverb "perfectly" is appropriate here (note that the suffix "ly" is the only addition to the previous sentence).*
Acceptable:	*The new paint was a perfect match with the old color.*
Reason:	*By rewriting the sentence, it is possible to retain the use of "perfect" as*

	opposed to "perfectly." In this variation, "match" is used as a noun instead of a verb (it is one of those words, such as "run," "walk" and "top," that can be used as either a noun or a verb). Since "match" here is a noun, then the appropriate word to modify it is an adjective, "perfect."
Not acceptable:	*The guest vocalist sang beautiful.*
Reason:	*"Beautiful" is an adjective; here it is used incorrectly to modify a verb, "sang."*
Acceptable:	*The guest vocalist sang beautifully.*
Reason:	*As an adverb, "beautifully" is the correct modifier for the verb, "sang."*
Acceptable:	*The guest vocalist had a beautiful voice.*
Reason:	*An alternative to using an adverb is simply to reword the sentence.*
Not acceptable:	*He cooks good.*
Reason:	*"Good" is an adjective. Even though it is sometimes used as an adverb in informal speech, this is not acceptable in formal speech or writing.*
Acceptable:	*He cooks well.*
Acceptable:	*The results seem good.*
Reason:	*Here, "good" modifies the noun "results," not the verb "seems."*

Double Negatives

Most schoolchildren are taught at an early age that double negatives are not acceptable in either written or spoken English. Nevertheless, the use of double negatives is a common practice. Since it involves a basic grammatical principle, this error may attract more unfavorable attention than more troublesome but less widely understood issues. In other words, using double negatives can make you look bad, even to people who are far from grammatical experts themselves.

Simply defined, a double negative is the use of two negative terms (words such as "not" and "no") to modify the same word or phrase, as in this example:

I don't have no money.

The problem here is that the statement goes too far in expressing a negative concept. "Don't" (a contraction of "do not") indicates that the speaker is without money, and then "no" is also used to make the same point.

For the statement to be correct, one of the negative words must be dropped. Each of the following versions makes the desired point in an acceptable manner:

I have no money.
I don't have any money.

In addition to "not" and "no," other negative words include the following:

none
hardly
scarcely
neither
nor
any contraction ending in "n't" (words such as didn't, couldn't, hadn't, wasn't, and weren't)

"Scarcely" and "hardly" may be less obvious than the other examples, but they are indeed negative words. It would be incorrect to say "scarcely no rain" or "hardly no mistakes," for instance. Instead, the preferred construction would be "scarcely any rain" or "hardly any mistakes."

On the other hand, "neither" and "nor" may be used together, *if* they are not modifying the same thing, as in the following:

Neither Lisa nor David noticed the broken window.

This is not a double negative, because each negative term modifies a different noun. "Neither" applies to Lisa, and "nor" modifies David.

Whenever you describe something in negative terms, be sure to avoid the problem of double negatives. If you are unsure, carefully consider the logic of what is being said. If a negative concept is expressed once within a sentence, it does not need to be repeated.

Inappropriate Comparisons

Another common mistake is using the incorrect word to make comparisons. This is sometimes a problem when using the comparative degree (that is, when two items, persons, etc., are being compared), and perhaps more frequently when forming the superlative degree (when the comparison involves a group of three or more).

The main points to remember include the following:

1) Be sure to use the correct degree (comparative or superlative).
2) Do not use double comparatives or superlatives, or otherwise overdo any comparison.

For many adjectives (especially those consisting of just one syllable), the comparative degree involves the addition of "er," while the superlative degree calls for "est," as in these examples:

Kristin is *short* (no comparison made).

Kristin is *shorter* than Elaine (comparison between two persons, or comparative degree).

Kristin is the *shortest* girl on the basketball team (comparison among more than two persons, or superlative degree).

The living room is *cold* (no comparison).

The living room is *colder* than the kitchen (comparative degree).

The living room is the *coldest* room in the house (superlative degree).

For most adverbs and for many adjectives with several syllables, these relationships are indicated not by adding "er" or "est" but by placing "more" or "less" in front of the word (for the comparative), or "most" or "least" for the superlative. Some examples include:

Good sportsmanship is important (no comparison).

Good sportsmanship is more important than ability (comparative degree).

Good sportsmanship is the most important of all traits (superlative degree).

Jenny was not careful (no comparison).

Jenny was less careful than Deborah (comparative degree).

Jenny was the least careful member of the club (superlative degree).

For those words using "er" or "est" to show comparisons, it is not necessary, and actually grammatically incorrect, to use "less," "least," "more," or "most." This represents a repetition of the same concept, and thus is not acceptable. Some examples of such redundancy are as follows:

Not Acceptable	Acceptable
most funniest	funniest
more faster	faster
more colder	colder
most larger	largest

Some adjectives and adverbs take neither "more," "most," "less," or "least" nor the addition of "er" or "est." Instead, a different form is used to indicate each degree. Some of the most common of these words include the following (each is followed by the comparative and superlative form):

far (farther, farthest)
good (better, best)
bad (worse, worst)
little (less, least)

These forms are less common than other types of comparisons, and should be remembered to avoid errors.

For some adjectives, the concept of comparison does not exist. These are known as absolute adjectives. Examples include "empty," "fatal," "perfect," and "round." An accident can be fatal, but not "more fatal" or "less fatal." Instead of a comparative or superlative form, a word such as "almost" or "nearly" can be used to modify an absolute adjective (as in "almost empty").

FOUR

WORKING WITH VERBS

Any effort in speaking or writing involves the use of verbs. Verbs are words we use to express action, and as such include some of the most powerful expressions in the English language (such as "win," "kill," "love," "hate," "attack," "give," and many others). Verbs also express existence or being (such as "is," "am," and other forms of the verb "to be"), as well as occurrence (such as "happen").

Some verbs function as auxiliary, or helping, verbs, where they combine with other verbs to form phrases such as "am waiting," "was living," and "does care," where "am," "was," and "does" are the helping verbs. Other labels may be ascribed, to verbs to describe them more completely, but the intent here is to keep the matter as uncomplicated as possible.

Not only does the English language include a wide variety of verbs, but most verbs come in several different forms (such as past tense, present participle, past participle, and so forth). As a result, the use of verbs can be complex, and opportunities for errors are numerous.

To simplify matters, this chapter will not list scores of verb forms and discuss their intricacies in great detail. Instead, it will focus on some of the major errors made in the use of verbs, and how to avoid them.

Anyone can achieve basic mastery of verbs and verb phrases by following these steps:

1) Be able to use the principal parts of verbs with confidence.
2) Learn to be consistent with verb tenses.
3) Avoid misunderstanding about verb definitions.

USING THE PRINCIPAL PARTS OF VERBS

A weakness that appears too often in some people's language is using the principal parts of verbs incorrectly. The phrase "principal parts" refers to these three forms:

Present
Past Tense
Past Participle

The present may be considered the simplest form of any verb. It consists of the infinitive, but without the word "to" being necessary (examples of infinitives include "to run," "to hit," and "to love"). Here are the present forms of some commonly used verbs:

ask
build
cheat
do
find
talk

The past tense usually involves a variation of the present, either through the addition of "d" or "ed," or through another change in the word. For the verbs listed above, the past tense is as follows:

asked (addition of "ed")
built ("d" changed to "t")
cheated ("ed" added)
did ("o" changed to "id")
found ("i" replaced by "ou")
talked ("ed" added)

The past participle normally includes one or more auxiliary, or "helping," words as shown below:

was asked
had built
has cheated
had done
was found

For many verbs, switching from the present to the past tense, or making any similar change, is quite simple. For others, the process can become complicated by the fact that changes are not always made in the same way.

For what is known as "regular" verbs (which are in the majority), the switch to past tense is made by adding "d" or "ed" to the present form. Usually, words that end in "e" in the present tense (such as "fake," "like," and "smile") require only the addition of "d."

In using regular verbs, one common mistake is dropping the necessary "d" or "ed" in the past or past participle form. This can be the result of simple carelessness, or it might be due to the misleading sound of certain words rather than any mistaken logic. For example, the verb "ask" sounds almost the same in the present as in the past tense, but it is important that the "ed" suffix not be left out. This may not be obvious in oral communication, but it can result in a more serious error in written work. Here are some examples of such errors, which should always be avoided:

Not acceptable: *President Bush ask Congress to enact the legislation as soon as possible.*

Acceptable: *President Bush asked Congress to enact the legislation as soon as possible.*

Not acceptable: *After the operation, she really look bad.*

Acceptable: *After the operation, she really looked bad.*

Not acceptable: *Wally use to be a great pitcher.*

Acceptable: *Wally used to be a great pitcher.*

Not acceptable: *I was not suppose to be there.*

Acceptable: *I was not supposed to be there.*

A different challenge arises in using words known as "irregular" verbs. These are verbs for which the past tense and past participle are formed not by adding "d" or "ed," but by changing the words in different ways—or, in a few cases, by leaving them unchanged for all three principal parts.

The difficulty with irregular verbs is that no single rule exists that can be applied in forming the past tense or past participle. For some, this process involves adding the suffix "en" (as in changing "give" to "given" or "fall" to "fallen"). For others, internal vowels are changed (examples include "bleed" being changed to "bled," and "fight" being changed to "fought"). For some words that end in "d," the final letter is changed to "t" (as in changing "bend" to "bent" or "send" to "sent"). But some words (such as "cut" and "set") remain the same in the present, past, and past participle form.

Some irregular verbs pose problems more commonly than others. For example, consider the principal parts of "teach":

teach
taught
taught

Even though the past tense and past participle differ markedly from the present form, these are widely known even by people with marginal grammatical skills. A phrase such as "she teached me" or "he had teached the same skills to three generations of quarterbacks" rings untrue, and is not likely to be encountered frequently.

For some irregular verbs, however, mistakes are more commonplace. Otherwise simple words such as "begin," "come," "do," and "go" can cause confusion due to inconsistencies in the way the past tense or past participle is formed. Here are some examples:

Not acceptable: *He begun the job late.*
Acceptable: *He began the job late.*
Not acceptable: *Her grandmother's health had began to decline.*
Acceptable: *Her grandmother's health had begun to decline.*
Reason: *The principal parts are "begin" (present), "began" (past), and "had begun" (past participle). "Begun" should never be used without a helping verb; anytime it appears alone, a mistake is in the offing. Similarly, "began" stands alone. An auxiliary verb such as "had" or "have" should not be used in conjunction with the past tense, "began."*

Not acceptable:	The salesman come by yesterday.
Acceptable:	The salesman came by yesterday.
Not acceptable:	He had came to our house before.
Acceptable:	He had come to our house before.
Reason:	For the irregular verb "come," the correct change to the past tense is the switch of the vowel "o" to "a," resulting in "came." For the past participle, however, the correct word is the same as for the present tense, "come." This is a different pattern than the one cited above for the verb "begin," but such is the nature of irregular verbs. Luckily, they are in the minority, and their principal parts can be memorized without undue difficulty.
Not acceptable:	He done a good job.
Acceptable:	He did a good job.
Reason:	With many writers or speakers, the incorrect use of "done" instead of "did" is more a matter of habit or carelessness than lack of understanding. Nevertheless, this error should be avoided. The past tense is "did." The past participle, "done," should always be supported by a helping verb.
Not acceptable:	Maria had went to the store.
Acceptable:	Maria had gone to the store.
Reason:	The past tense of "go" is "went," and the past participle is "gone." "Went" should never be accompanied by an auxiliary or helping verb.

The following table lists the three forms of common irregular verbs:

Table 4-1

Twenty Commonly Used
Irregular Verbs

Present	Past	Past Participle
be	was	been
become	became	become
begin	began	begun
blow	blew	blown
choose	chose	chosen
drink	drank	drunk
eat	ate	eaten
fly	flew	flown
give	gave	given
have	had	had
hit	hit	hit
kneel	knelt	knelt
lay	laid	laid
lie	lay	lain
see	saw	seen
set	set	set
sit	sat	sat
swim	swam	swum
teach	taught	taught
throw	threw	thrown

(Note: For the correct usage of "lie," "lay," "sit," and "set," see chapter 6.)

Tense refers to the way in which verbs express time. Is an action happening now? Has it already happened? Did it take place at one specific time, or over an extended period? Is it something that has not yet happened, but that is projected for the future? These and other such matters are clarified by the use of different verb tenses.

Verbs can have any of the following tenses:

Present
Past
Future
Present perfect
Past perfect
Future perfect

Here is an example of how a verb can be expressed in different tenses:

Present: *Ray plays golf (happening now or habitually).*

Past: *Ray played golf (action that has already taken place).*

Future: *Ray will play golf Tuesday (has not yet taken place).*

Present perfect: *Ray has played golf since childhood (action completed over an indefinite period of time).*

Past perfect: *Ray had played golf the day the earthquake hit (action completed before another action took place).*

Future perfect: *Ray will have played golf ten times by the end of the week (action that will take place in the future before another action will take place).*

Verbs can also be expressed in what is known as the progressive form. This involves the addition of the suffix "ing" along with the use of "is," "am," "was," or some other form of the verb "to be." For example, the present progressive tense of the verb above would be, "Ray is playing golf." The past progressive version would be "Ray was playing golf." Other progressive forms would follow similar patterns.

In using verb tenses correctly, the key word is consistency. Tense should be consistent within single sentences as well as within passages consisting of a number of sentences. The careful writer avoids shifting from one tense to another unnecessarily. Here are some examples of this principle:

Not acceptable: Sarah looked at me and starts crying.

Acceptable: Sarah looked at me and started crying.

Reason: The first verb, "looked," covers something that took place in the past. For the sake of consistency (and simple logic), the verb that follows should also be in the past tense ("started") rather than the present ("starts").

Not acceptable: In his guest article in the Washington Post, Congressman Murphy spells out some of the reasons he decided to run for president. He lists four basic issues of particular concern. Mr. Smith says that all of these issues have been ignored by the current administration.

Acceptable: In his guest article in the Washington Post, Congressman Murphy spelled out some of the reasons he decided to run for president. He listed four basic issues of particular concern. Mr. Smith said that all of these issues have been ignored by the current administration.

Acceptable: In his guest article in the Washington Post, *Congressman Murphy spells out some of the reasons he decided to run for president. He lists four basic issues of particular concern. Mr. Smith said that all of these issues have been ignored by the current administration.*

Reason: The writer can treat the article in the past tense, as in the first sentence of the first example, but if that is the case, the verbs in each sentence that refer to the article should also be in the past tense. If Congressman Murphy "spelled out" reasons, then the next sentence should show that he "listed" issues. In the following sentence, "said" should be used instead of "says" to maintain consistency. The second example shows these changes.

The writer can also treat the article as something that continues to exist now, and in so doing use the present tense. That is the writer's choice. If the present tense is used at the start of the passage, though, it should continue to be used in the sentences that follow. Thus, "list" should be used instead of "listed," and "says" should appear in the third sentence rather than "said."

The main principle is that once a tense has been selected, the writer (or speaker) should be consistent in use of that tense in the same sentence or passage.

MISUNDERSTANDING THE MEANINGS OF VERBS

Another area of frequent misunderstanding concerns the basic meaning of a verb. This is not only a problem for people with limited grammatical skills but also for those who are attempting to expand their vocabularies. Students who have read widely, for instance, often begin using words that are new to them. A danger in this practice, however, is using such words incorrectly.

For example, consider the following statements:

The lady had impeachable taste.
He believed the witness was procrastinating; she had lied to him before.

What the writer of the first sentence probably meant was not "impeachable" but "impeccable." The verb "impeach" has to do with accusing someone, as in impeaching the president. "Impeccable," on the other hand, means flawless or perfect.

In the second sentence, the intended word is probably "prevaricating," which means violating the truth. "Procrastinating" means putting things off, or delaying.

Another type of misunderstanding involves words that sound much the same. For example, "adapt" is often confused with "adopt." "Emigrate" is mistakenly used for "immigrate," and vice versa.

To avoid such misunderstandings, take the following steps:

1) Make sure you have access to a good dictionary, and use it frequently. Whenever you

are unsure about the meaning of a verb (or any other word, for that matter), look it up in the dictionary and make sure you understand its usage.

2) Consult the list of frequently misused words in chapter 6. Try to commit to memory any that you feel might appear in your own speech or writing.

3) Read widely. By reading books, articles, stories, or other material, you can observe a variety of verbs in action. Do not be afraid to add some of them to your own vocabulary. If possible, underline interesting verbs that catch your attention; then look them up in the dictionary to develop an understanding of their meaning and correct usage.

FIVE

USING NOUNS AND PRONOUNS CORRECTLY

A solid grasp of the rules of grammar and usage must include an understanding of how to use nouns and pronouns effectively. These are among the basic building blocks that make up our language.

"A noun is a person, place, or thing." Do you remember this definition from elementary school? Some grammarians consider this to be a definition that is too simplistic or narrow in focus, but it does apply to the majority of nouns. Most words that function as nouns serve as identification labels for people, places, or things. For example, typical nouns include the following:

dog	house	baseball
wine	sky	tool
man	girl	Susan
lake	country	England

In addition to these types of nouns, others fall outside such a narrow definition. For instance, just what constitutes a "thing?" In a broad definition, this can also include abstract concepts such as love, hatred, and fear—all of which are also nouns. In addition, some words that also serve as other parts of speech can also function as nouns. For example, in the statement "running is his favorite sport," the word "running" functions as a noun rather than a verb.

Pronouns represent a different category of words. They act as substitutes for nouns, often providing a means for avoiding repetition. For example, consider the following passages. The first is presented without pronouns, while the second makes use of two common pronouns.

> *Marsha took Marsha's car to the shop. Marsha had never dealt directly with a mechanic before. Marsha was surprised at the mechanic's uncooperative manner of talking to Marsha.*
> *Marsha took her car to the shop. She had never dealt directly with a mechanic before. She was surprised at the mechanic's uncooperative manner of talking with her.*

Without words such as "she," "her," and other pronouns, much discourse would be annoyingly repetitive. In addition to helping achieve variety, pronouns can indicate possession, show relationships to other words, and clarify a writer's intent, among other functions. This relatively small group of words plays an important role in the communication process.

It is extremely important to understand the basic nature of nouns and pronouns. After all, these words serve as the subjects of sentences, among other functions, so using them correctly is necessary in building sentences that are grammatically correct. In addition, a basic understanding of how nouns and pronouns function helps in avoiding problems such as errors in agreement.

UNDERSTANDING CASE

The word "case" refers to the way nouns and pronouns function within a sentence. Some languages have a large number of cases, but English has only three: subjective, objective, and possessive. (Note: The subjective case can also be called the nominative, and the possessive may be called the genitive.) Even with just three cases, the rules here can seem a bit tricky, and remembering just how to use the right form may be challenging. For example, have you ever had difficulty deciding whether to use "who" or "whom"? Nevertheless, by mastering a few basic concepts, you can handle this type of problem with competence.

The subjective case is used when a noun or pronoun serves as the subject. The objective case applies when the noun functions as an object. Put simply, the subject serves as the source of action, while the object receives the action or in some other way acts as a recipient.

Table 5-1

Case Forms for Selected Pronouns

Pronoun	Subjective	Possessive	Objective
I	I	my, mine	me
he	he	his	him
she	she	her, hers	her
we	we	our, ours	us
they	they	their, theirs	them
who	who	whose	whom

Quite often, speakers or writers become confused when choosing the correct case to use—especially for those pronouns that vary in form in the subjective, objective, and possessive cases. This is an area that may separate students with marginal grammatical skills from those with greater capabilities. If you can master use of this relatively small number of words, your grammatical skills can be improved substantially.

Table 5-1 lists some case forms of special interest. Study them and try to commit them to memory.

Following are some examples of the factors involved in selecting the proper case.

Not acceptable: *David and me are going to the store.*
Acceptable: *David and I are going to the store.*
Reason: *"Me" is the objective case of "I," not the subjective. Since the subject of the sentence includes the speaker, "I" is the proper form.*

An easy way to make certain your choice is correct would be to isolate the subject you are not sure of—in this case, "me"—and see if the case form you have used sounds right. Here, that would mean removing "David" from the sentence as well as the conjunction "and," and then changing the verb to its singular form to match a singular subject. The result would be as follows:

Me am going to the store.

This obviously violates the rules of grammar. "I am going to the store" makes more sense. "David and I are going to the store" simply builds on this basic thought.

Not acceptable: *Please give your advice to Sharon and I.*

Acceptable:	*Please give your advice to Sharon and me.*
Reason:	*In this sentence, "me" rather than "I" should be used, because "Sharon and I" are receiving the advice, not giving it (the objective versus subjective case). As noted in the previous example, a good way to check this would be to isolate the pronoun in question, and then determine if the selection seems appropriate. "Please give your advice to I" is obviously incorrect; "me" is the proper choice.*
Not acceptable:	*Peg and her will be here soon.*
Acceptable:	*Peg and she will be here soon.*
Acceptable:	*She and Peg will be here soon.*
Reason:	*The subjective case ("she") is appropriate here. The pronoun refers to someone who will be acting, not a recipient of the action.*
	In the second acceptable example, the order of "Peg" and "she" has been reversed; to some, this may sound less awkward than the sequence in the previous example.
Not acceptable:	*Teddy and myself fixed the broken radio.*
Acceptable:	*Teddy and I fixed the broken radio.*
Reason:	*The subjective case is correct. "Myself" would not even be the form used in the objective case; instead, "me" would be appropriate if the action were reversed, as follows:*

The radio was fixed by Teddy and me.

"Myself" is properly used to relate to the pronoun "I" rather than replace it, as in "I myself did not believe it would work" or "I hurt myself."

Not acceptable: *Rita is the person who I mentioned yesterday.*

Acceptable: *Rita is the person whom I mentioned yesterday.*

Reason: *"Whom" should be used in this instance, because it is the object of the word "mentioned." "Who" would be the correct choice if it were the subject, as in "Who killed the cat?"*

The use of "who" and "whom" can be tricky. Remember that the proper form for the subjective case is "who," and "whom" is used in the objective case. The distinctions between the two are not as strictly observed as they once were, but it is still a good idea to be aware of the difference. If you feel uncertain about using "who" or "whom" in any given situation, do not overlook the option of rewording your statement so that neither is used. For example, you might consider this alternative to the statement above:

This is Rita. I mentioned her to you yesterday.

PRONOUN-ANTECEDENT AGREEMENT

As discussed in chapter 2, proper agreement is one of the most important principles of grammar. Not only is it important that subjects and verbs agree but, so too should pronouns and the words to which they refer.

66

Anytime a pronoun is used, it should agree with its antecedent (that is, the word or words that come before it). Here are several examples:

Not acceptable: *A student should never forget to do their homework.*

Acceptable: *A student should never forget to do his homework.*

Acceptable: *Students should never forget to do their homework.*

Reason: *If a pronoun refers to a singular noun, it should also be singular. In this example, "student" is singular, so "their," a plural pronoun, is not correct. A singular pronoun, "his," is needed.*

An alternative would be to use a plural noun ("students") and then follow it with a plural pronoun ("their"). This is shown in the third statement. A particular advantage to this approach is that it eliminates the question of gender. Some people feel the use of "his" to refer to people of both sexes discriminates against women. This belief often leads to the use of awkward phrases such as "his or her" or, even worse, "his/her." Making the noun and pronoun plural helps avoid this problem.

Not acceptable: *Each of the boys used their own personal equipment.*

Acceptable: *Each of the boys used his own personal equipment.*

Acceptable: *The boys used their own personal equipment.*

Reason: *The pronoun here refers to "each," not to "boys," which is the object of a*

prepositional phrase. Since "each"
is a singular noun, a singular pro-
noun ("his") is appropriate.

The noun and pronoun can also
be made plural ("boys" and "their")
to achieve agreement.

Collective nouns require special attention when it
comes to pronoun-antecedent agreement (a collective
noun is one that refers to a group, such as "committee,"
"herd," or "jury"). If the group is acting as a single unit,
the collective noun would be considered singular, and
any pronoun that refers to it should also be singular. If
elements or members of the group act separately, the
subject would be considered plural, and a plural pronoun would be used, as shown below:

Acceptable:	*The jury reached its verdict.*
Acceptable:	*The jury couldn't agree on their ver-dict.*
Acceptable:	*The members of the jury couldn't agree on their verdict.*
Reason:	*In the first example, the jury is acting as a whole, and as a result "jury" can be treated as a singular noun. A sin-gular pronoun ("its") is therefore ap-propriate.*

In the second example, jury
members are acting separately (this
is made apparent by the fact that
individual members disagreed with
one another). Thus, a plural pronoun
("their") is needed. The third exam-
ple avoids any confusion by making
the noun in question "members," a
word that is clearly plural.

Another good practice in using pronouns is to make certain there is no confusion regarding which word is being referred to by a pronoun. This is more a matter of precision than of grammatical correctness, but is nevertheless worth considering. The following examples illustrate this principle:

Not acceptable: *Sheila's sister lent us her calculator.*

Acceptable: *Sheila's sister lent us Sheila's calculator.*

Acceptable: *We borrowed Sheila's calculator from her sister.*

Reason: *In the first version, "her" is unclear. Is it Sheila, or her sister? The second version clarifies this question. The third version changes the wording substantially; one advantage is that it is not necessary to repeat the name "Sheila."*

Not acceptable: *Nancy called Amy three times while she was in Europe.*

Acceptable: *While she was in Europe, Nancy called Amy three times.*

Acceptable: *Nancy called Amy from Europe three times while she was there.*

Reason: *In the initial version, it is unclear whether it was Nancy who was in Europe, or Amy. The second and third versions eliminate any confusion about the reference being made by "she."*

MASTERING GOOD USAGE

Even when you master the basic rules of grammar, it is still possible to make a bad impression or to hinder communication by using words improperly. Correct usage, on the other hand, not only improves communication but shows you are competent in this key aspect of language skills.

"Usage," as noted in chapter 1, refers to the selection and use of words. "Good" usage involves not just using words in a way that conforms strictly to their definitions but also selecting the appropriate level of formality given the nature of the audience and the general situation at hand. "Good" usage can help you achieve the following:

- Clear communication
- Conformity with standards expected of educated people
- The confidence that comes with a sure command of the language
- A reduction in the chance that your intentions will be misunderstood
- Improved prospects for making a positive impression on the reader or listener

"Bad" or inappropriate usage, on the other hand, can lead to problems. These include:

- Misunderstanding on the part of the reader or listener
- The impression that you are incompetent in the use of language
- The possible appearance that you lack good judgment in using terms appropriate to the situation or the audience
- An overall lack of effectiveness that can offset other positive qualities

In the extreme, improper usage is often the target of humor. Characters in movies and television situation comedies, who are portrayed as lacking in intelligence, for example, often have problems with usage.

FORMAL VERSUS INFORMAL USAGE

The English language operates at different levels of formality. A conversation in a locker room, for example, will probably be less formal than one taking place in a classroom or at a highly structured business meeting. The same may true of a friendly letter to a close friend or relative, as compared to a research paper or a letter applying for a job.

The use of abbreviations and contractions, for instance, is more common in informal usage than in formal situations. A note to your cousin will probably include words such as "I'll" instead of "I will" or "I shall," and may even use incomplete sentences, abbreviations, or slang words. A letter from one business official to another, on the other hand, will avoid such features.

In some cases, standard rules of grammar and usage can be bent or broken without undue damage.

In fact, this can sometimes be effective. A college president with a Ph.D. was recently heard to say "Ain't no way!" when questioned if an academic program would be eliminated. His choice of words gave extra emphasis to the message, perhaps in part because it contrasted so strongly with the formality one would expect of a highly educated person in a scholarly setting.

While informal language can be effective in some situations, it is highly inappropriate in others. As noted in Chapter One, many judgments may be made about you that are based at least in part on your command of written or spoken language. A sure command of what is often known as standard English is essential.

A person who holds a solid mastery of formal or standard English can always slip into informal usage if desired. But the opposite is not necessarily true. To illustrate this principle, consider the options of a tennis player. An excellent tennis player may need all of her skills to defeat an opponent of roughly equal ability and experience. If she plays against a raw beginner, the full extent of her capabilities will not be needed, and she can reduce her effort significantly and still win the match. The player with limited skills, however, cannot suddenly upgrade her level of play to that of a tennis champion.

A similar situation applies to grammar and usage. If you achieve a high level of skill in formal English, you can always drop back to informal usage whenever the situation might seem appropriate. At the same time, you will always be prepared to meet generally accepted requirements for "standard" usage when the need arises.

COMMON USAGE WEAKNESSES

Many usage weaknesses could be avoided if the speaker or writer only thought about what is being said.

Here are some of the most common:

"*Hopefully.*" This word should not be used as a substitute for "potentially" or "it is hoped." Rather, its primary meaning relates to acting in a hopeful way, as "she gazed hopefully at the clouds." Expressions such as "hopefully, the economy will improve" or "hopefully, you won't be too late" violate traditional standards.

"*Literally.*" If used correctly, this word is not a problem. But, too often, it is used incorrectly, as in the following example:

> *The opposing team literally blew them off the field.*
> *Rick literally laughed his head off.*

In these two statements, the term "literally" is intended to describe something that is short of reality. "Literally," though, does not mean "figuratively." It means something is actually true as stated. The speaker or writer who makes such statements is saying things that would, in truth, be impossible to take place. For the second sentence to be true, Rick's head would actually have to fall off!

A simple way to avoid this mistake is to use another word such as "nearly." A sentence such as "Rick nearly laughed his head off" would be understood as using figurative language, and would not belie the real meaning of "literally."

"*Most unique.*" This term is often used to describe unusual items, as in "it is the most unique specimen available." But unique means *one of a kind*, so it is impossible for anything to be more unique than anything else. It either *is* unique, or it isn't. This mistake can be avoided simply by remembering what unique actually means, and then noting that a modifier such as "most" does not make sense in connection with the word.

"*One of the only.*" This may sound acceptable until you think carefully about it. "Only" in this context hints at singularity, but, if such is the case, the other words become superfluous and "only" could stand on its own. If you are really trying to say that the item is only one of several, then the preferred phrase would be "one of the few" or "one of only four" (or whatever number applies), with the word "only" used to modify the number in question.

"*Ubiquitous.*" This word means being everywhere at the same time, or omnipresent. For example, God might be described as ubiquitous, or a supernatural creature in a work of fiction might be depicted in this way. It does not mean "common." Therefore, referring to "the ubiquitous automatic teller machine" or some other common item is stretching the meaning of the term.

SOME COMMON USAGE CHOICES

In many instances, effective usage involves making the right choice between two possible words or phrases. If the wrong word or phrase is selected, the effectiveness of the writer or speaker can be greatly diminished.

The following pages list some of the word choices that most frequently cause mistakes. To avoid such errors in your own communications, take these steps:

1) Read this section carefully.
2) Review your own work and see if you have been guilty of making poor choices. If you are a student, look through some English compositions, old term papers, or other written assignments. Once you identify your own particular weaknesses, you can take steps to remedy them.
3) Commit to memory as many of the examples listed as possible. That way, you will be

prepared to make correct choices in future efforts, both in written and spoken communications.

Selected Usage Choices

Accept vs. Except. "Accept" is a verb meaning to receive, among other definitions. "Except" is used as a preposition or conjunction denoting exclusion, as in the following:

Acceptable:	*I am pleased to accept the job.*
Acceptable:	*Everyone except José failed the test.*
Acceptable:	*He would win twenty games, except for the fact that he is a lousy pitcher.*

Adapt vs. Adopt. "Adapt" means to adjust. An animal might adapt to its environment, or an engineer might adapt an instrument for a new purpose. "Adopt" means to take as one's own, as in a couple adopting a child or a company adopting a new logo.

Advice vs. Advise. "Advice" is a noun, and "advise" is a verb. One might advise a friend to give up smoking; a suggestion to that effect would be advice.

Alot vs. a lot. The use of "alot" is never acceptable. The only correct term is the two-word expression, "a lot." Even this is considered to be informal, however, so it should not be utilized too frequently in written work.

Alright vs. All right. In formal usage, "all right" should always be employed. "Alright" is generally considered to be non-standard usage.

Among vs. Between. These words fulfill similar functions, with usage determined by the number of persons or things involved. Generally, "between" applies to two, and "among" refers to three or more.

Acceptable:	*The secret stayed between the two of them.*

>*Acceptable:* The money was divided equally among the four winners of the lottery.

In recent years the distinction between both words has become blurred, and it is not necessarily an error to use one of these words in place of the other, depending on the circumstances. But following this long-standing practice is generally preferred; in that way you meet the standards of what some might call traditionalists or purists where usage is concerned.

Allude vs. Elude. "Allude" means to refer to something; an example would be "one writer alluding to the work of another." "Elude" means to escape or keep from being caught, as in "a criminal eluding the police."

Comprise vs. Constitute. These words refer to elements of a whole, but as viewed from different perspectives. "A baseball team comprises infielders, outfielders, catchers, and pitchers" (in other words, it includes them). It is incorrect to say that "infielders, outfielders, catchers and pitchers comprise a baseball team" (just as it is incorrect to substitute the phrase "makes up" for "includes"). Instead, one would say these players constitute a baseball team.

Data vs. Datum. In a strict sense, "datum" is singular, and "data" is plural. Some people feel it is incorrect to say "the data is clear," for example, preferring instead "the data are clear." Usage of the word "data" for both the singular and plural has become common, however, and "datum" is not frequently used. This could be considered a matter of personal choice, but you should be aware that the traditional usage is still followed by some, and it could be considered an error to confuse the singular and plural.

Elicit vs. Illicit. "Elicit" means to bring out or cause, as in eliciting a response from a teacher. "Illicit" means forbidden or in violation of the law. An example would be a publication that is considered illicit because it violates obscenity laws.

Emigrate vs. Immigrate. "Emigrate" means to leave one country for another. "Immigrate" means to come into a country to live there. A person from Poland might *emigrate from* that country; he would *immigrate to* his new home in another nation.

Fewer vs. Less. These words are often confused. The best way to distinguish between the two is to remember that "fewer" refers to numbers, while "less" applies to general descriptions of quantity or amount. If something can be actually counted, use "fewer," as in "fewer than twenty-five people attended." If a number cannot be attributed, use "less," as in "she eats less food than before" or "the less said, the better."

Good vs. Well. "Good" is an adjective, while "well" is an adverb. The former should be used in describing nouns and pronouns, while the latter applies to action.

Acceptable:	*Linda is a good singer.*
Not acceptable:	*Linda sings good.*
Acceptable:	*Linda sings well.*

Impact vs. Affect. "Impact" is a noun. It is often used incorrectly as a verb, but should never appear as such in formal writing or speech. Instead, a verb such as "affect" should be used.

Acceptable:	*The budget cuts will have an impact on every citizen in the county (here, "impact" is a noun).*
Acceptable:	*The budget cuts will affect every citizen in the county.*
Not acceptable:	*The budget cuts will impact every citizen in the county.*

Infer vs. Imply. Both of these refer to meanings that are conveyed indirectly but should not be used interchangeably. The person conveying information *implies*; the person receiving the information *infers.*

Acceptable: The coach implied that he would let Raul play.

Acceptable: Raul inferred that the coach was planning to let him play.

Lay vs. Lie. These words are often used mistakenly, especially in the past tense or past participle form. "Lay" in the present tense refers to placing an object somewhere, as to lay a ticket on a counter. "Lie," on the other hand, includes among its definitions the act of lying down, as to lie on a bed or sofa. Neither word can be substituted for the other, although, since the past tense of both verbs is spelled and pronounced "lay," confusion often arises. Here are some examples of correct usage:

Acceptable: She wanted to lie on the new sofa.
She yawned and then lay down on the bed.
She had lain on the worn mattress many times.
She is lying on her side with a glass of juice in her hand.

Please lay your books on the table.
He laid the gun on the shelf.
Someone had laid two decks of cards on the table.
The girl in the grass skirt is laying flowers at the feet of everyone who gets off the ship.

Note: One way to remember the difference is to note that "to lay" and its princi-

pal parts usually involve an item that receives action. For instance, one might lay a coin or a photograph on a table; "coin" and "photograph" are items that receive the action of "laying."

Me vs. Myself. Some writers and speakers assume that "myself" is somehow more formal than "me." In fact, "myself" should only be used to clarify or emphasize the word "I" or "me" in a sentence, as in "I kicked myself" or "I myself have never seen a flying saucer." Avoid the incorrect use of "myself" as a replacement for "me," as in "My husband and myself will attend." The correct form is "My husband and I will attend."

Principal vs. Principle. "Principal" means major (for example, "greed might be a principal factor in one's decision to commit a crime") or head (as in "the principal of a school"). A "principle" is a belief or truth (as in "the principles on which our nation was founded").

Real vs. Really. The two should not be used interchangeably. "Real" should not be used as an adverb or as a synonym for "very."

Acceptable: *This is real sugar.*
Not acceptable: *It was a real good story.*

In formal usage, "really" means actually (not "very"), as in "He really ate the whole pizza!" In colloquial language "really" has come to mean "very," as in "she is a really good swimmer." But such usage should be limited to informal communication.

Regardless vs. Irregardless. "Irregardless" is one of those words that is best left out of one's vocabulary. It is sometimes used as a variation of "regardless," but only the latter is considered truly acceptable.

Respectively vs. Respectfully. These words have

79

two distinct meanings. Use "respectively" to indicate the order of items in a list or series. "Respectfully," on the other hand, means having or showing respect.

Acceptable: The comments were made by Tom, Elaine and Donald, respectively.

Acceptable: The student spoke respectfully of a professor he admired.

Set vs. Sit. "Set" means to place something somewhere. "Sit" is used when you mean "to sit down." These two words should never be interchanged. To help remember the difference, keep in mind that "set" usually takes an object; in other words, something must receive the action that is taking place, as in this example:

Acceptable: Mike, please set the computer on the desk.

Here, the computer is the recipient of the action being performed by the subject of the sentence, Mike.

That vs. Which. Both of these words may be used to lead into clauses. If the clause is restrictive (that is, if it is essential to the meaning of the phrase that it modifies), the word "that" should be used. If it is a non-restrictive clause (one that can be deleted without altering the meaning of what is being modified), use "which."

Examples:

The food that she loves most is pizza. (If "that she loves most" were deleted, the sentence would have an entirely different meaning. Thus, "that" is the better choice.)

Walking, which is becoming increasingly popular, is a great form of exercise. (If "which is *a great form of exercise" were deleted, the basic thought would still be the same, even though an amplifying comment had been removed. Accordingly, "which" should be used).*

An easy way to make this distinction is to pay attention to the use of commas. If a clause is set off by commas, as in the second example, use "which." If a clause is not set off by commas, use "that."

Their vs. There. "Their" is a possessive pronoun, while "there" is most often used as an adverb, as in these examples:

The lions protected their young.
Put the food there.

Make sure that one of these words is not carelessly used in place of the other.

Who vs. Whom. Using "who" or "whom" can be tricky. The main thing to remember is that "who" is used in the subjective case, and "whom" in the objective. In other words, "who" should generally be used when it is doing the action, and "whom" when it is receiving the action.

Examples:
Who will win the contest? ("Who" is the subject of the sentence).
Whom should I blame? ("I" is actually the subject here; "whom" is the recipient of the blame).

The same is true of the words "whoever" or "whomever." If the pronoun is in the objective case, "whom," or "whomever" should be used. Otherwise, "who" or "whoever" is appropriate.

Worse vs. Worst. "Worse" describes comparative degree, while "worst" describes the superlative. Thus, one should use "worse" in comparing two items, and "worst" in comparing three or more, as in these examples:

Acceptable: *Ed's cold is worse than Dawn's.*
Acceptable: *The Bears are the worst team in the league.*

SEVEN

WHERE TO GO FROM HERE

This book has been offered as an overview of the most important principles of acceptable grammar and usage. The reader is invited to use the information provided as a starting point for improvement in this vital area.

After reading this book, however, you might wonder: what next? This concluding chapter addresses the question of how to follow up in making improvements in your own use of grammar.

USE THIS BOOK AS REFERENCE

Some books are meant to be read once and then set aside. This text is designed to have the same ease in reading, but it can also be retained for future reference.

If you are serious about improving your own use of grammar, take the time to reread the previous chapters until you can remember all of the basic points covered. Then keep the book handy for future use as you complete writing assignments, prepare oral reports, or do other work where questions of grammar must be considered.

An especially effective use of your time can be to

study examples of the serious errors discussed in Chapter Two. Then call them to mind, or consult the information covered, when a related question arises.

MEMORIZE RULES AND EXAMPLES

The need to memorize countless rules about grammar has long been a reason why some people experience a lack of success in this area. If this has been the case in your own past, do not give up. Instead, take the time to commit to memory the most basic facts at hand, such as those presented in earlier chapters.

This is something anyone can accomplish with a little effort. One way to approach the process is to make up your own memory aids. If you have trouble remembering a rule, develop an example you can use as a mental guide. Here are some examples:

Suppose you keep confusing the correct usage for "advice" versus "advise." You know that one is a noun and the other is a verb, but sometimes forget which is which. By thinking in terms of alphabetical order, you can solve this problem. The letter "c" comes before "s" (the only letters in these two words that are not the same), and the "n" in noun comes before the "v" in verb, alphabetically speaking. Once this relationship is established, you can always remember that "advice" is the noun (what is given or received) and "advise" is the verb (the act of giving advice).

To remember what comma splices are, make up and memorize an example such as "Comma splices are bad, they should never be used." As an example of a problem with subject-verb agreement, memorize a phrase such as "Agreement mistakes is bad" or "Agreement are important." Do the same for other major points of grammar. You can make the examples as blatant or silly as you like, but the main object is to remember the rules as easily as possible. After committing a few such examples to memory, you can recall them as needed when speaking, writing, or editing material you have written.

CONSULT OTHERS

When considering questions about grammar, consult others who may be of assistance. For example, team up with a fellow student and work out a deal to check rough drafts of each other's work for mistakes when this practice is allowed at your school.

Another approach would be to have a sample of your writing reviewed by someone who is qualified to judge the effectiveness of your grammar. This could be a teacher, a friend who is a college English major, or anyone else with a high level of competence in this area. If any weaknesses are pointed out, work on them until a) you fully understand what you have done wrong, and b) can come up with appropriate improvements.

TAKE ADVANTAGE OF EDUCATIONAL OPPORTUNITIES

As you take required English courses at the high school or college level, make the most of them. Even if the courses are not among your favorites, they represent an organized, intensive experience that can enable you to make great strides in this crucial area of personal development.

In addition, consider taking a specialized class or two in grammar. Many community colleges, for instance, offer non-credit or pre-college courses in the fundamentals of grammar that are open to anyone, including high school students or even those not enrolled in school at all. Such a course can be well worth any time you devote to it. Some classes can even be taken on an independent basis, where you work at your own pace, using a workbook or—better yet—a personal computer.

FOUR PARTING TIPS FOR SUCCESS

Here are four tips for success in your own mastery of English grammar:

1) *You are already well on your way.* If you can speak and write the English language, you are already well on your way to success. Improving skills in grammar is not a matter of starting "from scratch." Instead, you probably already know more than 90 percent of what is needed to have first-rate skills in this area. After all, how many years of experience do you already have in speaking and writing English? What is needed for most people is not years of intensive study and practice but just some fine-tuning of skills you already have.

2) *Nobody expects you to know it all.* Even though most people already understand most of the basics of grammar (or we would not be able to communicate with one another), some of the rules are complicated. Even "professionals" such as college professors, high school teachers, and writers often find it necessary to consult reference books or check with a colleague about a particular rule or practice. There may be a few so-called "walking encyclopedias," who know everything there is to know about grammar and usage, but they surely must constitute an extremely small minority!

Unless you plan to make your living as some kind of grammatical expert, no one will expect you to memorize every obscure term or complicated rule about the finer points of grammar. All that is needed is a basic level of competence as outlined in this book. This means adhering to generally accepted standards for an educated person in contemporary society, but you do not need to have a flawless understanding of every nuance of grammar. You must be willing to work hard to achieve this level, but you won't need to devote your life to the study of grammar.

3) *Mistakes can be corrected.* Even if you make a mistake, it is not carved in stone. This is particularly true with written material. If you take the time to check any written work you have produced, you can detect and correct errors that might occur due to simple carelessness or the pressures of deadlines. You can also consider alternative choices if you are uncertain about a specific rule of grammar.

This same kind of care and forethought is also possible in spoken communication, although to a lesser degree. A good practice is to speak slowly enough so that questions of grammar can be considered. For instance, say you are speaking before a group, or are talking with a potential employer. You want to mention that you and a friend had an interesting conversation that morning. As you start to verbalize this thought, you must make a quick decision. Do you say "my friend and I" or "my friend and me"? An alternative might be to avoid the choice entirely. A statement such as "I was talking with a friend this morning" can be used to resolve your uncertainty of the "I versus me" question.

4) *Improving your skills is worth the trouble.* Remember this: People judge you, at least in part, by the way you speak and write. Do you plan to go to college? Hope for a scholarship? Want a good job? Care how you are regarded by others? If such matters are important to you, then mastery of effective skills in grammar should also be a top priority. So good luck in making the most of your efforts in this vital area!

GLOSSARY

Adjective. A word used to modify nouns or pronouns.

Adverb. A word used to modify verbs, other adjectives, or adverbs.

Case. A grammatical concept used to indicate the role that a noun or pronoun plays in relation to the verb in a sentence. (In English we have two cases: subject and object. Latin has six.)

Clause. A phrase containing a subject and a verb.

Comma splice. A grammatical error resulting when two main clauses are joined by a comma.

Conjunction. A word used to connect words or groups of words.

Determiner. A function word used to mark a noun. (Examples in English include: *the, a/an, some, this, my.*)

Fused sentence. The result of joining two sentences without punctuation or connecting words.

Gender. A grammatical concept used to determine nouns, pronouns (and in some languages, adjectives) as being masculine, feminine, or neuter. (In English, *he/him* is masculine, *she/her* is feminine, and *it* is neuter.)

Grammar. The rules that govern the way in which

words are put together (also, the overall results of applying those rules).

Independent clause. A clause that can function on its own as a sentence (also known as a main clause).

Intransitive (verb). A verb that does not take a direct object. (Examples in English are: *to arrive, to fall, to die.*)

Main clause. See *Independent clause.*

Noun. A person, place, thing, or concept.

Person. A grammatical concept used to describe a verb's subject as being first (*I*), second (*you*), or third (*he/she/it*) person.

Preposition. A function word used to introduce a phrase. (Examples of prepositions in English include: *to, from, for, with, without.*)

Pronoun. A word that substitutes for a noun (such as *I, me, her, him*)

Run-on sentence. See *Fused sentence.*

Sentence fragment. A grammatical error that results from using an incomplete sentence instead of a complete one.

Subordinate clause. A clause that cannot stand on its own as a sentence, but is dependent on a main or independent clause.

Syntax. The rules a language employs to combine words into phrases, clauses, and sentences.

Transitive verb. A word used to indicate action (may also indicate existence or occurrence).

Voice. A grammatical concept that refers to whether the action of the verb is performed by the subject (in which case the verb is in the *active* voice) or whether the action is performed to/on the subject (in which case the verb is in the *passive voice*).

Examples:

Verb in active voice: *Henry ate the sandwich.*

Verb in passive voice: *The sandwich was eaten by Henry.*

ℱOR FURTHER READING

Azar, Betty. *Understanding and Using English Grammar*. Englewood Cliffs, N.J.: Prentice-Hall, 1989.

Bromberg, Murray, and Julius Leibb. *The English You Need to Know: Reading, Writing, Grammar*. Hauppage, N.Y.: Barron's, 1987.

Diamond, Harriet, and Phyllis Dutwin. *Grammar in Plain English*. Hauppage, N.Y.: Barron's 1989.

Fiske, Robert. *Webster's New World Guide to Concise Writing*. New York: Prentice-Hall, 1989.

Fowler, Henry. *A Dictionary of Modern English Usage*. New York: Oxford University Press, 1987.

Greenbaum, Sydney, and Janet Whitecut. *Longman Guide to English Usage*. White Plains, N.Y.: Longman, 1989.

Hodges, Hohn C. et al. *Harbrace College Handbook*. New York: Harcourt Brace Jovanovich, 1990.

Strong, William. *Basic Usage and Vocabulary*. New York: McGraw-Hill, 1983.

Strunk, William, Jr., and E. B. White. *Elements of Style*. New York: Macmillan, 1979.

$\mathcal{I}$NDEX

ABOUT THE AUTHOR

Mark Rowh holds bachelor's and master's degrees in English and a doctorate in education. He has taught English classes in two-year and four-year colleges, and currently serves on the administrative staff at New River Community College in Dublin, Virginia. Dr. Rowh is highly experienced not only in teaching English but also in applying the principles of effective grammar and usage to the creation of reports, proposals, brochures, and other written materials. He is the author of more than one hundred magazine articles and nine other books, including *Coping with Stress in College*, published by College Board Books.